CAKE POPS

CAKE POPS

Delightful cakes for every occasion

Francis van Arkel

NH
NEW
HOLLAND

Contents

FOREWORD

Cake Pops—a new hype or here to stay? I think they will be around for a while, as cake pops—in every shape, size and colour—are so much fun and easy to make. And super yummy too!

These bite-size cakes are a treat in every sense of the word.

You don't need a lot to get started, in fact you will probably have most equipment at home. We don't use complicated cake recipes in this book and are happy for you to use ready-made cake mixes.

Besides teaching you how to make various simple cake pops, we also show you how to make the more complicated types, which do require some additional tools and ingredients. For these recipes, some creativity also comes in handy.

As soon as you know how to make the cake pops in this book, you're ready to start creating your own designs. Cake pops never get boring and always taste good. And no-one, young and old, will be able to resist one

of these great looking cake pops. You can use various types of cake and frosting. That's what cake pops are: a mixture of cake crumbs and frosting or butter cream. That is why they are so creamy and easy to make. Then the fun starts: decorating your cake Pops.

In this book, we not only make cake pops, but also cake balls, cake bonbons, cupcake bonbons and cupcake pops. The basic recipe for these treats is very similar to that for cake pops. The introduction explains the differences between the various types.

You probably want to get started making your cake pops now. Happy cake popping!

Francis van Arkel

INTRODUCTION

In this book, we'll be making cake balls, Cake Pops, cupcake pops, cupcake bonbons and cake bonbons. The basics are almost the same, but they 'look' very different. All of them are based on cake crumbs mixed with frosting or butter cream. This mixture is rolled into cake balls, which are dipped into candy melts. Cake Pops are the same, but are placed on a stick, and sometimes have a different shape. The difference with cupcake pops is that they are shaped like a cupcake and are, of course, beautifully decorated. Cupcake bonbons look like small pralines in the shape of a cupcake, and cake bonbons speak for themselves: they look like pralines, but are much quicker to make. We provide you with the basic recipes for all five types, plus examples of how to finish and decorate them.

What do you need?

To get started with the Cake Pops, you only need a few ingredients. You will probably have most of these and the necessary kitchen appliances at home. Otherwise everything is easily available in the supermarket or store. The only thing you will probably have to buy in a specialist cake store, or via the Internet, are candy melts (large chocolate drops) and lollipop sticks and in some cases modelling paste or marzipan with tylose (or gum). If you want to start making cupcake pops and cupcake

bonbons, you will need cutters and bonbon moulds. Below is a list of the things you need.

KITCHEN EQUIPMENT:
Oven, cake tin, baking spray, two baking sheets, greaseproof paper, toothpicks or cocktail sticks, electric mixer, spray, squeeze bottle, large mixing bowl, microwave-proof bowls, metal spoon, cling film.

INGREDIENTS FROM THE SUPERMARKET:
Cake mix (plus the ingredients necessary according to the package to make the cake), ready-made frosting, cake decorations (sprinkles and candy).

SPECIALIST INGREDIENTS AND TOOLS:
(Flower) cutter, lollipop sticks, candy melts, bonbon moulds, edible ink pens, food colouring and oil-based flavourings, floral

foam or Styrofoam, modelling paste or marzipan with tylose. Most of these are available at kitchen ingredients stores or gourmet ingredients stores.
EXTRA TOOLS:
For those with some experience in cake decorating, I have also included Cake Pops and other treats you can decorate with the cake decorations you already have. The possibilities are endless. You can use all types of cutters, your sugar-craft gun, glitters, sprinkles and much more.

Before you start

Make sure you have everything ready, weighed and counted. You should have a baking sheet with grease-proof paper at the ready to dry your pops, and have the decorations on your worktop, so you can add the sprinkles before the candy melts have gone hard. Don't forget to open up the decoration packaging. This saves a lot of time and annoyance! Put the decorations in little bowls, for ease of use: this is the easiest way to roll the Cake Pops in glitter. Do you need to halve the chocolate drops? Then cut these in half before you start. It is also important that you bake the cake the evening before you want to make the pops. Chill the cake overnight, to make it easier to work with.

Baking the cake

The cake is the basis for all your Cake Pop treats. To start with, you can use a ready-made cake mix from the supermarket. It doesn't matter what brand you use, although the amounts can differ per brand. For the recipes, I'm using 450g (15oz) of cake mix. The cake has been baked according to the instructions on the box. For the best results, use a 25x25 cm (10x10 inch) cake tin. You can of course use your own cake recipe, but I enjoy cake mix as it is always constant. You can also add flavours to the cake mix. Make sure the cake chills overnight, so that it is easier to crumble.

Making the cake balls

Crumble the cake with your hands or in a food processor. In both cases, you have to ensure you get very fine crumbs, so work the crumbs until there are no big bits left. Rub two bits of cake together between your hands until you only have crumbs left. If a larger piece falls off, pick it up and rub it into crumbs again.

To make a smooth cake ball mix, I add 300-330g (10½-11oz) of ready-made frosting or butter cream to the crumbs. Mix the two with a metal spoon; the easiest way is to hold the spoon with the rounded side down. Keep pushing and stirring until you have a smooth and creamy mix, which is not too sticky. I prefer using the food processor to crumble my cake. Don't put the entire cake in at once, but process it in batches. As soon as you have the cake crumbled, tip everything in the food processor and add the frosting. Mix these up by pressing the pulse button a few times. As a rule, use light-coloured frosting for a light-coloured

cake, because they will combine into a homogenous mix. If the cake and frosting have been mixed and the resulting mix is too wet, the balls will fall apart. In that case, add a bit more cake to the mix.

Did you run out of cake? A ready-made supermarket cake comes in handy! With my basic recipe, you can make 55 small balls. This is the size I like best and the one I used in the recipes in this book. I take a spoonful of the mixture and squeeze it into a ball gently (I prefer to wear plastic gloves when rolling the balls). Then I weigh the ball, making sure each one weighs 20g (⅔oz). This way, all the balls look the same, making for a pretty display. While I'm squeezing the balls, I also lightly roll them into a ball shape. Leave the balls to dry on the grease-proof paper on the baking sheet.

Candy melts

Candy melts are large chocolate drops. They are available in many different colours and very easy to use: you only need to melt them. You can melt them in two ways.

In the microwave:
Pour the candy melts in a large microwave-proof plastic bowl and heat them at 360W for about 5 minutes. Stir the melts and then put them back in the microwave for 30-45 seconds at a time, again at 360W. Keep stirring and melting until you have a smooth mass. Make sure the chocolate does not become too hot, and keep it away from water! Once it's melted, it's melted.

In a double-boiler:
If you haven't got a microwave, this is an good alternative. Put a pan of water on the stove and bring to the boil. Place a bowl over the pan and pour in the candy melts. Keep stirring the candy melts until they are soft and glossy.

Using melted candy melts

Chances are that you will be using several colours of candy melts at once. How do you keep all those different portions of melts melted? A hot plate comes in handy; whether it's electric or you can use tea lights. Pour the melted candy melts in smaller bowls—still big enough to dip your Cake Pops in—and keep them warm on your hot plate. You can also pour the melts in a fondue bowl, if you have one.

Sometimes the melted candy melts are a bit thick, making them hard to work with. Never dilute candy melts with water; the mass will go lumpy and becomes unusable, which is a shame. If necessary, always dilute candy melts with a bit of solid vegetable fat such as margarine. Add the fat bit by bit until you have achieved the right consistency. Never use liquid vegetable fat or oil: this will not go hard and ruin the coating.

Candy melt colours

Candy melts are available in many different colours and you can buy them in most stores. You can mix your own colours by combining various colours of candy melts. Red and blue make purple, so mix up equal parts of candy melts and add a bit more from either colour until you end up with the colour you want. You can also add food colouring to your candy melts. In that case, only use white candy melts. Not every food colouring is suitable: make sure you use an oil-based type. Wilton has four basic colours (red, blue, green and yellow), which is good enough to get you started, but there are lots of other oil-based colourings available from other brands.

Most candy melts taste of vanilla, but you can even vary that by adding your own flavourings. Again, use oil-based flavourings.

Coating the cake balls

The cake balls have to be firm, but not frozen. About 15 minutes in the freezer is enough. If they're frozen, the candy melts coating will harden too quickly, and the layer will be very uneven. Although the candy melts should be fluid, it should not be too liquid or hot. It's a case of practising until you get it right. But don't worry, you will! Don't roll the cakes through the coating, but dip them in, to avoid getting crumbs in the candy melts.

Sometimes a light-coloured coating is used in combination with a dark cake, and the dark layer still shows through. In that case, just dip the cake twice.

The best result is a Cake Pop with a beautifully smooth, even candy melt coating. It is easier than it looks! Use bowls which are deep enough to dip (at least 7cm/¾inch) and make sure the coating is thin enough to dip the cake in easily. The coating should run off as soon as you lift the cake ball out. If the coating is too thick, you can dilute it with some vegetable fat (add a little bit at a time!). Tap off the extra coating while swivelling the Cake Pop around. There's a method for each cake to achieve a smooth coating.

Coating cake balls and cake bonbons

Make sure the cake balls have been properly chilled in the fridge or have been left in the freezer for a maximum of 15 minutes. For cake bonbons, press the cake balls into the bonbon mould. Chill them, and then remove them from the mould. Carefully place a cake ball or cake bonbon in the coating and then spoon some of the coating over the ball or bonbon. Remove the ball or bonbon with a fork, tapping the handle of the fork against the edge of the bowl to remove any excess coating. Place the ball or bonbon on a baking sheet, lined with greaseproof paper. If the coating gets hard and a lot of coating leaks out the sides, 'cut' around the ball or bonbon with a cocktail stick and then leave the coating to set. The excess coating can, when set properly, be broken off, to create beautifully smooth cake balls or cake bonbons. Use a squeeze bottle or piping bag to decorate the cake balls or bonbons. If you want to decorate your cake balls or bonbons with sprinkles, you can add these as soon as you have placed them on the baking sheet. The sprinkles will then stick to the coating; if the coating has already started to set, they will fall off.

Coating the cupcake bonbons

Cupcake bonbons are slightly different from cake bonbons. Cake bonbons are made by pressing the cake balls in bonbon moulds, removing and then coating them. Of course they can be beautifully decorated with coatings in various colours, to make them

look like real pralines. Cupcake bonbons, however, are shaped like a cupcake and already look very festive like that. There are cupcakes in various shapes, some higher or narrower than the traditional types, and you can experiment with cupcake bonbons in a similar way. To create the characteristic ridges along the sides, you need special serrated bonbon moulds. These moulds can be quite hard to find. I managed to find an original mould at a wholesaler's, but you can also use the peanut butter cup moulds sold by cake supply stores; these are usually a lot cheaper.

Fill the moulds halfway with coating, and place the cake ball on top. Carefully push the ball into the mould; this way, it will be completely coated and get the desired ridges. Make sure the coating doesn't spill over the edge, so stop as soon as this threatens to happen. You will have to experiment with how much coating you have to use for the best results. Leave the bonbons to set in the mould and then remove them. Hold the cupcake bonbons at the coated side and then dip the other side into a candy melts coating (preferably a different colour). Remove the bonbons and let the excess coating

run off while holding the bonbons at an angle and swivelling them. Put the cupcake bonbon upright and immediately decorate it with sprinkles—before the coating has set. If you want to add other decorations, make sure the coating has set first.

There are other cupcake shapes as well and you can, of course, use whatever shape you like best. This makes your cupcake bonbons more special and festive. You can, for example, put the cupcake bonbons on a lollipop stick. This turns them into cupcake pops; how to coat these is described under 'Making and coating cupcake pops'.

Coating Cake Pops

Make sure the cake balls have been chilled well in the fridge or have been left in the freezer for a maximum of 15 minutes. Use a deep bowl for your coating, so you can dip in the Cake Pops. Dip 1-2cm (1in) of a lollipop stick into the coating and insert it into the Cake Pop, until about halfway. Allow to set for a few minutes, to ensure the cake doesn't slip off the lollipop stick when you hold it upside down. Dip the Cake Pop into the coating, ensuring it is fully covered, and remove it in one smooth, swivelling movement. Turn and tap off any excess coating by gently tapping the lollipop stick against the edge of the bowl. Keep swivelling the Cake Pop, to avoid the coating getting too thick in one spot. Put the Cake Pop right side up. If there is still coating running off the sides, you can remove it from the lollipop stick with your finger or a bit of kitchen towel. Keep swivelling the pop. It takes some time to do well: make sure you take your time as well, because this gives you the best results.

Sprinkles should be added straight away. Other decorations can be added when the coating has set.

Making and coating cupcake pops

Cupcake pops are usually coated with more than one colour. First you will have to turn the cake balls into cupcake pops. You can do this as follows. Take a chilled cake ball and roll it into a cylinder which is almost as big as a 3cm (1¼inch) flower cutter. Slot the cutter over the cake cylinder and make sure it gets filled with cake, without pushing the entire cake ball in—you need some of the cake for the top of the pop. As soon as the flower cutter has been filled, you can mould the bit that sticks out the top and make it nice and round. Carefully remove the cupcake from the cutter and put it back in the fridge. As soon as you have made small cupcakes out of all the cake balls and they have been chilled,

they are ready for coating. Dip each cupcake into the coating, up to the top of the ridge.

Remove the cupcake and keep swivelling it to remove the excess coating. Make sure you hold the cupcake at an angle. When the coating has started to set and spread, put the cupcake down upside-down on a baking sheet, lined with greaseproof paper, and carefully insert a lollipop stick, which you have also dipped in the coating. To be clear: you stick it into the side you just coated! Leave this coating to set. Pick up the cupcake by the stick and dip the rounded side into the second coating (preferably a different colour), all the way up to the edge of the first coating. Remove the cupcake, and keep swivelling it to remove excess coating, while holding it at an angle.

Use a cocktail stick to coat any bits that haven't been coated properly, or remove coating from where it shouldn't be. As soon as the coating has started to set, you can put it upright and start decorating—adding the sprinkles before the coating has completely gone hard. Allow the cupcake pop to set in a Styrofoam block.

You can, of course, also make these cupcake pops without inserting a lollipop stick. In that case, they're called cupcake bonbons: see 'Coating cupcake bonbons'.

Piping candy melts

Candy melts are perfect for decorating Cake Pops, bonbons and cupcakes. Scoop some of the melted candy melts into a small piping bag, with or without a tip. You can even make your own piping bag out of some grease-proof paper. A sandwich or freezer bag is a cheap alternative to a piping bag and works well. Scoop in some melted candy melts and squeeze it towards one of the corners. Snip off a tiny bit of the corner and start decorating.

Making your own cake

You can also make your own cake, instead of using ready-make cake mix. These are three of my favourite cake recipes.

Vanilla cake

250g (9oz) butter
250g (9oz) granulated sugar
5 eggs
250g (9oz) self-raising flour
2 tspn of vanilla extract

Beat the butter and sugar until soft and fluffy, using a hand mixer or food processor. Add the eggs one by one and keep mixing until you have a smooth and light mix. Add the flour and vanilla extract and mix until you have a smooth batter. Pour the batter into a greased square baking tin (25x25 cm or 10x10in) and bake the cake in a preheated oven for 55-60 minutes at 160°C (325°F).

Chocolate cake

250g (9oz) butter
250g (9oz) granulated sugar
5 eggs
250g (9oz) self-raising flour
2 tspn of vanilla extract
2 tbsp cocoa, sieved

Beat the butter and sugar until soft and fluffy, using a hand mixer or food processor. Add the eggs one by one and keep mixing until you have a smooth and light batter. Add the flour, vanilla extract and cocoa and mix until you have a smooth batter. Pour the batter into a greased square baking tin (25x25 cm or 10x10in) and bake the cake in a preheated oven for 55-60 minutes at 160°C (325°F).

Red velvet cake

200g (7oz) butter, at room temperature
300g (10½oz) fine sugar
2 eggs
2 tbsp cocoa, sieved
a pinch of salt
1 tbsp red food colouring
240ml (8fl oz) buttermilk
350g (12oz) plain flour, sieved
50g (1¾oz) corn flour (cornstarch)
1 tsp baking soda
1 tbsp vanilla extract
1 tsp (apple) vinegar

Beat the butter and sugar until soft and fluffy, using a hand mixer or food processor. Add the eggs and mix until you have a smooth and fluffy mixture. Mix up the cocoa, salt and food colouring and add to the butter mixture. Add small quantities of the buttermilk, flour and corn flour at a time and mix through. Mix the baking soda with the vanilla extract and the vinegar and add this to the batter. Fold through carefully. Pour the batter in a greased square baking tin (25x25 cm) and bake the cake in a preheated oven for 55-60 minutes at 160°C (325°F).

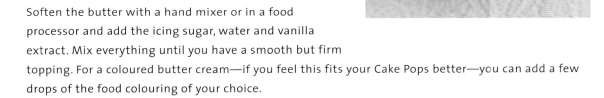

Making the butter cream and frosting

You can easily make your own cream and frosting. The ready-made types are easy to use, but—to be honest— the home-made variety tastes much better!

Vanilla butter cream

175g (6oz) butter, at room temperature
350g (12oz) icing sugar (confectioner's)
3 tbsp boiling water
a few drops of vanilla extract

Soften the butter with a hand mixer or in a food processor and add the icing sugar, water and vanilla extract. Mix everything until you have a smooth but firm topping. For a coloured butter cream—if you feel this fits your Cake Pops better—you can add a few drops of the food colouring of your choice.

Chocolate butter cream

175g (6oz) butter, at room temperature
350g (12oz) icing sugar
3 tbsp boiling water
a few drops of vanilla extract
4 tbsp cocoa, sieved

Soften the butter with a hand mixer or in a food processor and add the icing sugar, water, vanilla extract and cocoa. Mix everything until you have a smooth but firm topping.

Meringue butter cream

50ml (2fl oz) water
150g (5oz) granulated sugar
3 egg whites
250g (9oz) butter, at room temperature
a few drops of vanilla extract

Bring the water and 125g (4oz) of sugar to the boil. Keep stirring the mixture. Any sugar crystals that stick to the sides can be pushed down with a wet pastry brush. Stop stirring when the syrup comes to the boil and leave to boil for 5 minutes. In a bowl, beat the egg whites into almost stiff peaks, add the remaining 25g (¾oz) of sugar and keep beating until the sugar has dissolved and the egg whites peak. Keep beating and add the sugar syrup to the egg whites; stir the mixture until it is lukewarm (7-9 minutes). Add the butter and vanilla extract and mix everything until the butter has been absorbed. Add a few drops of food colouring if you want coloured butter cream.

Egg white frosting

2 egg whites
350-400g (12-14oz) icing (confectioner's) sugar

Beat the egg whites with a hand mixer and bit by bit add the icing sugar. Keep adding icing sugar until you have a thick mixture. Keep beating on the lowest setting for 10 minutes, until you have a fluffy frosting. Depending on how you want to use it, you can make the frosting thinner or thicker, to make it easier to pipe on. For a coloured frosting, add a few drops of food colouring.

Sugar frosting

250-300g (9-11oz) icing (confectioner's) sugar, sieved
2-4 tsp water

Pour the sugar into a bowl and stir in a little bit of water at the time. Depending on how you want to use it, you can make the frosting thinner or thicker, to make it easier to pipe on. For a coloured frosting, add a few drops of food colouring.

Satin frosting

45g (1½oz) vegetable fat, such as margarine

4 tbsp lemon juice

350g (12oz) icing sugar

1-2 tbsp hot water

Melt the fat in a saucepan and take off the heat. Stir in the lemon juice and half of the icing sugar. Bring to the boil and leave to boil for 1 minute. Take the pan of the heat again and stir in the remaining icing sugar. Keep adding hot water until you have a thick, but still pourable frosting. Use the frosting immediately to cover the cupcakes. For a coloured frosting, add a few drops of food colouring.

Toffee frosting

100g (3½oz) butter, melted

125g (4oz) condensed milk

50g (1¾oz) granulated sugar

1 tbsp maple syrup

Pour the melted butter in a pan and stir in the condensed milk, sugar and maple syrup. Boil the frosting for 5-6 minutes. Keep stirring. Leave the frosting to cool down: it will then become thicker and easier to spread on. This frosting has a light golden colour.

Storing your Cake Pops

Because Cake Pops are coated with a layer of chocolate, they will not dry out very quickly. That is a big advantage. As you are working with fresh ingredients, the Cake Pops can go off. Don't store the Cake Pops in the fridge: if you then take the cakes out and let them warm up to room temperature, the chocolate coating will start to sweat. It is better to store the cakes in a storage container, separating them with kitchen foil. Store the container in a dry, cool and dark place. A basement is ideal. Attention: if you use butter cream, the Cake Pops have to be stored in the fridge!

You can wrap Cake Pops separately in small cellophane bags and tie them with a nice ribbon or bow. This way, they also look very pretty as party treats. Cake balls and cake bonbons can be stored in a storage container or jar.

Presentation

If you have made beautiful Cake Pops, you should, of course, also pay attention to presentation: otherwise all that hard work would be for nothing!

There are various ways to present your Cake Pops. You can paint small wooden boards and drill holes in them, just big enough to fit the lollipop sticks in. You can cut Styrofoam or into a shape and wrap it in colourful wrapping paper. Stick holes in the wrapping paper with a cocktail stick, to make it easier to insert the lollipop sticks.

It is also a cute idea to fill glasses, cups or (painted) flower pots with sugar, salt and/or decorative pearls, and then insert the lollipop sticks.

Cake and cupcake bonbons look very pretty on a tiered serving tray, colourful plates or whatever you can think of.

STRIPES CAKE BALL

Melt the candy melts in the colours you want to use to dip the cake balls in and decorate with. I used brown, pink and white.

Dip the cake balls into the candy melts and allow them to set. Scoop the candy melts in a piping bag and decorate the cake balls with stripes, swirls or diamonds. Allow the cake balls to dry.

INGREDIENTS

For 55 cake balls

1.2kg (3lb) candy melts
(total weight), in various colours
(at least 2)
55 cake balls

Also needed:
piping bag

BIRD IN A NEST CAKE BALL

Melt the blue candy melts. Dip the cake balls into the candy melts and allow them to set.
Push one heart into the front of the cake ball for the beak, one in the back for the tail and two in the sides for the wings.

Roll out 110 tiny black balls from the fondant or marzipan for the eyes and stick them onto the cake pops with a cocktail stick and some melted candy melts. Allow this to dry.

Melt the brown candy melts. Crumble up the cornflakes and stir through the candy melts. Scoop 55 heaps on the greaseproof paper and let this set. Place a bird on top of each heap using a drop of candy melts. Allow to set.

INGREDIENTS

For 55 cake balls

1.2kg (3lb) blue candy melts
55 cake balls
220 small edible hearts
25g (¾oz) black fondant or marzipan
400g (14oz) brown candy melts
100g (3½oz) cornflakes

Also needed:
cocktail stick
greaseproof paper

JAWBREAKER CAKE BALL

Melt the various colours of candy melts separately; use at least 2 colours to get the jawbreaker effect. Place the bowls with the different colours side by side and make sure you have an empty bowl at hand. Insert a cocktail stick into the cake balls.

Dip the cake balls in one of the colours of candy melts and hold it over the empty bowl.

While turning the cake ball, drizzle over the second colour of candy melts; let the excess drip off into the bowl. This gives a lovely jawbreaker effect.

Decorate the cake balls with sprinkles in matching colours before the candy melts set. Don't use too much sprinkles, or you'll lose the colour effect on the cake ball. Allow the cake balls to set by sticking it in the Styrofoam. As soon as the cake balls have dried, remove the cocktail sticks.

INGREDIENTS

For 55 cake balls

*1.2kg (3lb) candy melts (total weight),
   in various colours (at least 2)*
55 cake balls
coloured sprinkles

Also needed:
cocktail sticks
Styrofoam

BROWN BEAR CAKE POP

Melt the candy melts. Dip 2 cm (¾ in) of the lollipop sticks into the candy melts and push them halfway into the cake balls. Push two drop-shaped candies into each ball as ears. You can also use a bit of candy melts as 'glue'. Dip the cake pops, including the ears, into the candy melts and allow to set.

While these are drying, make 55 equal-sized brown balls out of fondant or marzipan and mould them into little snouts. Make 55 even smaller black balls out of fondant or marzipan for the noses and stick these on the snout with a cocktail stick and some candy melts. Prick a few holes in the snout with a cocktail stick. Attach the snout to the cake pop.

Make 110 tiny black balls for the eyes and attach these to the cake pops. Make 110 tiny brown balls out of fondant or marzipan, press them flat and attach these to the ears. Make sure they are significantly smaller than the ears themselves. You can draw on the mouth with some edible ink or food colouring.

Add a bow underneath the face using a cocktail stick, some brown candy melts and two hearts. Attach a small lip in the middle of the bow to make it look more realistic. You can also make a small bow out of coloured fondant or marzipan and attach this to the cake pop.

INGREDIENTS

for 55 cake pops

1.2kg (3lb) brown candy melts
55 cake balls
*110 edible drop-shaped candies
  for the ears*
*50g (1¾oz) brown fondant
  or marzipan*
*25g (¾oz) black fondant
  or marzipan*
*edible ink or food colouring
  (colour of choice)*
110 small edible hearts
55 small edible lips

Also needed:
55 lollipop sticks
cocktail sticks

CLOWN CAKE POP

Melt the candy melts. Dip 2cm (3/4in) of the lollipop sticks into the candy melts and push them halfway into the cake balls. Dip the cake pops into the candy melts and allow them to set.

In the meantime, make 55 equal-sized red balls out of fondant or marzipan, mould them into little noses and attach them to the face. Make 55 small black balls out of fondant or marzipan for the eyes and attach these with some candy melts and a cocktail stick. Attach the edible lips to the face with some candy melts and a cocktail stick. In the same way, attach 1 UFO-shaped candy on top of the cake pop, to make a hat. Cut the fondant or marzipan into thin strips to make hair. You can also use a garlic press to make fine hair. If you are an experienced cake decorator and own a sugarcraft gun, then you can also use that to make hair.

Roll out 200g (7oz) of fondant or marzipan (in a colour of your choice) thinly and cut out 2 hearts per cake pop to make bows. Stick the points of the heart together with some candy melts. Attach a small circle, flower or other shape (from fondant or marzipan) in the middle. Attach the bow to the cake pop with some candy melts.

INGREDIENTS

for 55 cake pops

1.2kg (3lb) white candy melts
55 cake balls
50g (1¾oz) red fondant or marzipan
15g (½oz) black fondant or marzipan
55 small edible lips
55 edible shaped candies for the hat
50g (1¾oz) orange fondant or marzipan
200g (7oz) fondant or marzipan, in a colour of your choice

Also needed:
55 lollipop sticks
cocktail stick
heart-shaped cutter
garlic press or sugarcraft gun

FISH CAKE POP

Melt the candy melts. Dip 2cm (¾in) of the lollipop sticks into the candy melts and push them halfway into the cake balls. Dip the cake pops into the candy melts and allow them to set. Roll out the fondant or marzipan thinly and cut out 55 larger hearts for the tail fin and 110 smaller hearts for the side fins. Score the hearts with a knife.

Push a heart into one side of the cake pop, sideways, to create a top and bottom lip. Make a small incision on the opposite side. Insert some candy melts in the cut (a cocktail stick is handy to use) and then push in the large tail fin.

Hold the cake pop to let the candy melts set slightly and wait until the tail fin is firmly attached. Attach the side fins with some candy melts.

Make 110 balls out of white fondant or marzipan and 110 even smaller balls out of black fondant or marzipan. Attach the black pupils to the white eyes with some candy melts.

Keep the eyes nice and round. Attach 2 eyes to each fish head.

INGREDIENTS

for 55 cake pops

1.2kg (3lb) candy melts (in a colour of your choice)
55 cake balls
150g (5oz) fondant or marzipan with tylose (gum or modelling paste), in a colour of your choice
110 small edible hearts
25g (¾oz) white fondant or marzipan
10g (⅓oz) black fondant or marzipan

Also needed:
55 lollipop sticks
heart-shaped cutters in two sizes
cocktail stick

MELTING SNOW CAKE POP

Melt the candy melts. Dip 2cm (¾in) of the lollipop sticks into the candy melts and push them halfway into the cake balls. Dip the cake pops into the candy melts and allow them to set.

Take a small spoonful of candy melts and scoop this over the cake pops. Pull or press the candy melts down with the spoon, to make it look like melting snow. Sprinkle over sugar glitter and allow to set.

INGREDIENTS

for 55 cake pops

1.2kg (3lb) white candy melts
55 cake balls
50g (1¾oz) edible white sugar glitter

Also needed:
55 lollipop sticks
spoon

GLITTER & GLAMOUR CAKE POP

INGREDIENTS

for 55 cake pops

1.2kg (3lb) pink candy melts
55 cake balls
150g (5oz) edible white sugar glitter

Also needed:
55 lollipop sticks
paper praline cases
greaseproof paper

Melt the candy melts. Dip 2cm (¾in) of the lollipop sticks into the candy melts and push them halfway into the cake balls. Dip the cake pops into the candy melts.

Fill a bowl with sugar glitter, lay the cake pops on top and sprinkle over more glitter. Set the cake pops upside down on some greaseproof paper and allow to set.

You can serve the cake pops in matching praline cases. I used pink candy melts here, because I love the combination with the white glitter. You can use any colour of candy melts and various colours of sparkling sugar to create different glitter and glamour effects.

INGREDIENTS

for 12 princes and 12 princesses

1.2kg (3lb) pink candy melts
48 cake balls
200g (7oz) pink fondant
  or marzipan
200g (7oz) blue fondant
  or marzipan
25g (¾oz) white fondant
  or marzipan
14g (½oz) black fondant
  or marzipan
24 small edible hearts
25g (¾oz) orange and/or
  white fondant or marzipan
edible pearls, in matching colours

Also needed:
peanut butter cup mould or small
cupcake bonbon mould
24 lollipop sticks
2 round cutters (15cm (6in) diameter
and a smaller one)
a garlic press or sugarcraft gun

PRINCE & PRINCESS CUPCAKE POP

Melt the candy melts. Fill the moulds halfway with coating, and place the cake ball on top. Carefully push it into the mould, to ensure it gets coated nicely and the cake gets a ridged edge. Make sure the coating doesn't spill over the edge, so stop as soon as this starts to happen. You will have to try out how much coating you need to spoon into the mould for the best results. Fill 24 cupcake shapes. Allow the cupcakes to set in the mould and then take them out.

Dip a small bit of the lollipop stick into the candy melts and completely insert it into and through the coated cupcakes. Place an uncoated cake ball on top, so that the lollipop stick is inserted halfway.

Dip the cupcake pops into the candy melts, tap off the excess and allow them to set.

You can now start decorating the prince and princess. I made them as follows:

For the princess, roll out pink fondant or marzipan and cut out a circle (15cm (6in)). Cut out a small circle in the middle, to be able to slot the dress over the head. Let the dress rest on the shoulders: the cupcake shape will create the dress shape. Decorate the dress as you want.

Do the same with blue fondant or marzipan to give the prince a royal coat.

Cut out a wedge and fold them back for the collar. Decorate the coat as you want.

Cut out a crown from the same colour fondant. Make eyes from the white and black fondant and attach these and the hearts (for the mouth) to the face with a cocktail stick and some candy melts. Make hair by cutting orange or white fondant or marzipan into narrow strips or squeezing it through a garlic press or sugarcraft gun. Attach the hair to the head, under the crown. Stick some edible pearls on the crown.

RATTLE CAKE POP

INGREDIENTS

for 55 cake pops

1.2kg (3lb) white candy melts
55 cake balls
1 box of pink or blue aniseed sprinkles
100g (3½oz) pink or blue fondant or marzipan

Also needed:
55 lollipop sticks
cocktail stick

Melt the candy melts. Dip 2cm (¾in) of the lollipop sticks into the candy melts and push them halfway into the cake balls. Dip the cake pops into the candy melts.

Fill a bowl with pink or blue aniseed sprinkles, place a cake pop on top and cover it with more sprinkles. Take the cake pop in your hand and gently squeeze the sprinkles in the candy melts. Allow to set.

Roll the pink or blue fondant or marzipan into 10g (⅓oz) balls. Make a hole in each ball with a cocktail stick, so that you can insert a lollipop stick. Insert the lollipop stick through the fondant ball and push the ball up to 3cm (1¼in) under the cake ball.

Give the ball a slight squeeze, to ensure it doesn't fall off the stick.

These cake pops are a fun treat at a baby shower. You can also add pink or blue ribbons with the name of the baby on it.

CRAZY DISCO CAKE POP

INGREDIENTS

for 55 cake pops

1.2kg (3lb) brown candy melts
55 cake balls
1 bag of rice candy,
  coarsely chopped

Also needed:
55 lollipop sticks

Melt the candy melts. Dip 2cm (¾in) of the lollipop sticks into the candy melts and push them halfway into the cake balls. Dip the cake pops in the candy melts. Sprinkle over the chopped rice candy. You have to work quickly before the candy melts set.

FLOWER FRENZY CAKE POP

INGREDIENTS

for 55 cake pops

1.2kg (3lb) candy melts
  (total weight),
  in the colours of your choice
55 cake balls
200g (7oz) fondant or
  marzipan in matching colours
edible pearls in matching colours

Also needed:
55 lollipop sticks
small flower cutters (set of 3)
cocktail stick

Melt the candy melts you want to use to dip the cake pops (melt them separately). Dip 2cm (¾in) of the lollipop sticks into the candy melts and push them halfway into the cake balls. Dip the cake pops into the candy melts and allow them to set.

Roll out the marzipan or fondant and cut out two sizes of flowers. Use a soft mat underneath and push down on the flower heart, to make sure the flower edges curl up slightly.

You can attach the flowers to the cake pops with a cocktail stick and some candy melts. Attach some edible pearls to the flowers in the same way.

KISSES CAKE POP

for 35 cake pops

*crumbled cake, mixed with
    frosting or butter cream*
1.2kg (3lb) red candy melts
*edible lacquer spray or
    edible glitter powder*

Also needed:
kiss shape moulds
35 lollipop sticks

Fill the moulds with the cake mixture and press down well. Chill the moulds in the fridge for an hour, then take the cake pops out.

Repeat this until you have used up all the cake mixture. Keep the kisses you have made in the fridge until you are ready to start dipping.

Melt the candy melts. Dip 2cm (¾in) of the lollipop sticks into the candy melts and push them halfway into the kisses. Dip the cake pops into the candy melts and allow them to set.

You can create a lip gloss effect by using lacquer spray.

NOUGATINE CAKE POP

INGREDIENTS

for 55 cake pops

1.2kg (3lb) brown candy melts
55 cake balls
1 x 150g (5oz) bag of nougatine

Also needed:
55 lollipop sticks

Melt the candy melts. Dip 2cm (¾in) of the lollipop sticks into the candy melts and push them halfway into the cake balls. Dip the cake pops in the candy melts (see Coating the cakeballs). Sprinkle the cake pops with nougatine before candy melts set.

GIFT-WRAPPED CAKE POP

Push the cake balls in the square cutter and press down. Make 55 similar-sized cubes. Chill the cubes in the fridge for at least an hour.

Melt the different colours of candy melts separately. Dip 2cm (¾in) of the lollipop sticks into the candy melts and push them halfway into the cubes. Dip the cake pops in the candy melts and allow them to set.

Roll out the fondant or marzipan thinly and cut out 4 narrow 10cm (4in) long strips per cake pop.

Use 2 strips as ribbons around the cube and use the other 2 to make a bow. Cut them into unequal lengths, fold the ends towards the middle and attach them with some candy melts. Stick the smaller bow on top of the larger one. Cut out 2 small circles per cake pop (use the tip of a piping bag) and attach these to the sides of the bow. Place the bow on top of the cube and attach it with some candy melts.

INGREDIENTS

for 55 cake pops

55 cake balls
1.2kg (3lb) candy melts
   (total weight), in various colours
   (at least 2)
100g (3½oz) fondant or marzipan
   (total weight) in the colours
   of your choice (at least 2)

Also needed:
square cutter (3x3cm, 1in)
55 lollipop sticks
small round tip

ICE-CREAM CAKE POP

Melt the different colours of candy melts separately. Dip 2cm (¾in) of the lollipop sticks into the candy melts and push them halfway into the cake balls. Dip the cake pops into the candy melts, 'drop' them into an ice-cream cone and allow them to set. It looks quite natural if some of the candy melts runs over the side of the cone.

Stick the rest of the cake balls onto a cocktail stick and dip these into the candy melts. Hold them upside down by the cocktail stick and push them against the cake ball on the lollipop stick. Press down firmly (some of the coating will run over onto the cake ball below) and remove the cocktail stick. Sprinkle some of the coloured sprinkles on top before the coating sets; this also conceals the hole made by the cocktail stick.

INGREDIENTS

for 25 cake pops

1.2kg (3lb) candy melts, in as
   many colours you want to use
   for the ice cream
50 cake balls
25 ice cream cones,
   with the bottom cut open
coloured sprinkles

Also needed:
25 lollipop sticks
cocktail sticks

MUSHROOM CAKE POP

Take 20g (2/3oz) of cake mixture and shape this into a mushroom. Repeat until you have used up all the cake. Chill the mushrooms in the fridge for an hour.

Melt both colours of candy melts separately. Hold a mushroom by the cap and dip the stalk into the melted white candy melts, all the way up to the cap.

Let the excess candy melts drip off. Turn it upside down and insert a lollipop stick. Allow the mushroom to set. As soon as the stalks have dried, you can hold the candy pop by the lollipop stick and dip the cap into the red candy melts. Again, let the excess candy melts drip off. Allow the mushroom to set completely.

Give the mushrooms some white spots using a cocktail stick and white candy melts.

INGREDIENTS

for 55 cake pops

*crumbled cake, mixed with
  frosting or butter cream (without
rolling the cake into balls)
500g (17½oz) white candy melts
700g (1lb, 12½oz) red candy melts*

*Also needed:
55 lollipop sticks
cocktail stick*

CACTUS CAKE POP

Take 20g (2/3oz) of cake mixture and shape this into a long cactus. Repeat until you have used up all the cake. Chill the cacti in the fridge for an hour.

Melt the candy melts. Dip 2cm (¾in) of the lollipop sticks into the candy melts and push them halfway into the cake pops. Dip the cake pops into the candy melts.

Push rice candy in the pop, to make it look like a proper cactus. You can also make a small flower from some fondant or marzipan and attach it on top.

INGREDIENTS

for 55 cake pops

*crumbled cake, mixed with
    frosting or butter cream (without
    rolling the cake into balls)*
1.2kg (3lb) green candy melts
1 bag of rice candy
*small piece of fondant or
    marzipan for the cactus flower,
    red or orange*

Also needed:
55 lollipop sticks

PARTY CAKE POP

Melt the colours of candy melts you want to use to dip the cake pops. Dip 2cm (¾in) of the lollipop sticks into the candy melts and push them halfway into the cake balls. Dip the cake pops into the candy melts and allow them to set.

Shape a small ball of fondant or marzipan into a party hat and decorate it with spots or stripes.

Make 110 small balls from the white fondant or marzipan, and 110 even smaller balls from the black fondant or marzipan. Make eyes by attaching the black balls to the white balls with a cocktail stick and some candy melts. Attach the eyes to the cake pop. Roll tiny sausages out of the red fondant or marzipan, shape it into a mouth and attach it to the face with some candy melts.

INGREDIENTS

for 55 cake pops

1.2kg (3lb) candy melts
    (total weight) in colours
    of your choice
55 cake balls
500g (17½oz) fondant or marzipan,
in matching colours
15g (½oz) white fondant or marzipan
10g (⅓oz) black fondant or marzipan
25g (½oz) red fondant or marzipan

Also needed:
55 lollipop sticks
cocktail stick

SUNFLOWER CAKE POP

Melt the candy melts. Dip 2cm (¾in) of the lollipop sticks into the candy melts and push them halfway into the cake balls. Dip the Cake Pops into the candy melts and allow them to set.

Roll out the yellow fondant or marzipan thinly and cut out 2 sunflowers for each Cake Pop. Scrunch up some aluminium foil and unfold it again, to get a wavy effect. Stick the 2 sunflowers together with a cocktail stick and some candy melts and allow this to harden on top of the aluminium foil. Shape the flower heart by squeezing a small ball of brown fondant or marzipan and making indentations with the blunt side of a cocktail stick. If you have a silicon flower heart mould, you can use that instead.

Attach the flower heart with a cocktail stick and some candy melts.

Roll out the green fondant or marzipan and cut out 110 leaves with a leaf-shaped cutter. Allow these to harden on the aluminium foil as well.

Attach a sunflower to the front of the Cake Pop. Use a large drop of candy melts to firmly attach the flower. Press the flower down firmly but carefully, until the candy melts have set.

Use some more candy melts to attach leaves on either side of the sunflower.

Allow the Cake Pop to set.

INGREDIENTS

for 55 cake pops

1.2kg (3lb) green candy melts
55 cake balls
500g (17½oz) yellow fondant
  or marzipan with tylose (gum or
modelling paste)
500g (17½oz) brown fondant
  or marzipan with tylose (gum or
modelling paste)

500g (17½oz) green fondant
  or marzipan with tylose (gum or
modelling paste)

Also needed:
55 lollipop sticks
cutters (45 mm),
leaf cutter
aluminium foil
cocktail stick

BUTTERFLY CAKE POP

For each butterfly, create 5g (1 teaspoon), 10g (⅓oz) and 15g (½oz) balls from the cake mixture. Chill the balls in the fridge for at least an hour. Melt the candy melts. Dip 2cm (¾in) of the lollipop sticks into the candy melts and push through the 5g ball. Add the 10g (⅓oz) ball on top and finally insert the stick halfway into the 15g (½oz) ball.

Make sure there are no gaps between the cake balls and stick them together with some candy melts if necessary. Dip the cake pops into the candy melts and allow them to set. In the meantime, roll out the fondant or marzipan in the colours selected and cut out 70 larger hearts (for the wings) and 70 smaller hearts. Cut the small hearts in half. Stick 2 half hearts on each large heart. Attach the wings to the back of the cake pop with some candy melts. Hold the wings until the candy melts have set.

Make 70 small black fondant or marzipan balls for the eyes. Attach these to the face of the butterfly with some candy melts. Cut the liquorice into 2-3cm (¾-1½in) pieces. Dip one end into the candy melts (preferably white) and allow to harden. Make two holes in the top of the head, large enough for the liquorice. To give the butterfly antennae, dip the uncoated end of the liquorice into the candy melts and push this end in the holes.

INGREDIENTS

for 35 cake pops

crumbled cake, mixed with frosting or butter cream (without rolling the cake into balls)
1.2kg (3lb) candy melts (total weight) in colours of your choice
200g (7oz) fondant or marzipan with tylose (gum or modelling paste) (total weight), in the colours of your choice
10g (⅓oz) black fondant or marzipan
4 liquorice laces

Also needed:
35 lollipop sticks
heart-shaped cutters in two sizes
cocktail stick

BLUE BLOOD CUPCAKE BONBON

INGREDIENTS

for 55 cupcake bonbons

800g (28oz) red candy melts
55 cake balls
400g (14oz) white candy melts
150g (5oz) butter cream,
*   coloured with blue food*
*   colouring*
edible orange glitters

Also needed:
peanut butter cup mould or
*   small cupcake bonbon mould*
piping bag with star tip

Melt the red candy melts. Fill half of the mould with coating and put the cake ball on top. Carefully press the ball into the mould, to coat it with the candy melts and give it a nice ridge. Make sure the coating doesn't spill over the edge, so stop as soon as this starts to happen.

You will have to try out how much coating you need to spoon into the mould for the best results. Allow the cakes to set in the mould and then take them out.

Melt the white candy melts. Hold the cupcake bonbons by the red, coated side and dip the top into the white coating, up to the red edge. Keep turning the cupcake while letting the excess coating drip off. Put the cupcake bonbon right side up and allow to set.

Spoon the blue butter cream in a piping bag and add a decorative swirl on top of the cupcake. Sprinkle over some orange glitter.

GOLD AND SILVER CUPCAKE BONBON

INGREDIENTS

for 40 cupcake bonbons

crumbled cake, mixed with
  frosting or butter cream
  (without rolling the cake
  into balls)
1.2kg (3lb) white candy melts
edible silver powder
edible gold powder
20 silver stars
20 gold stars

Also needed:
mini cupcake moulds
cocktail stick
soft brush
greaseproof paper

Fill each hollow of the mini cupcake moulds with 25g (¾oz) of cake mixture and repeat until you have used up all the cake. Chill the cakes in the fridge for an hour. If you cannot use all the cake mixture in one go (if, for example, you only have one cupcake mould), then remove the bonbons from the mould after one hour and make new cupcakes. Put any cupcakes that are ready back in the fridge to chill.

Melt the candy melts. Coat the cupcake bonbons by placing them in the candy melts, covering them with some more candy melts and then lifting them out with a fork. Tap the fork handle against the edge of the bowl to remove excess candy melts. Allow the bonbons to set on a sheet of greaseproof paper. Cut away any excess coating with a cocktail stick. As soon as the coating has set, you can break off any extra bits.

Use a soft brush to cover half of the cupcake bonbons with silver powder, and the other half with gold powder. Attach the stars with a small drop of candy melts.

MARRAKECH CAKE BONBON

INGREDIENTS

for 55 cake bonbons

*crumbled cake, mixed with
  frosting or butter cream (without
  rolling the cake into balls)*
1.2kg (3lb) dark blue candy melts
blue edible sugar
55 edible silver pearls

Also needed:
*bonbon mould, preferably a
  silicone mould*
greaseproof paper
cocktail stick

Fill each hollow of the bonbon moulds with 15-20g (½--⅔oz) of cake mixture and repeat until you have used up all the cake. Chill the bonbons in the fridge for an hour. If you cannot use all the cake mixture in one go (if, for example, you only have one mould), then remove the cake bonbons from the mould after one hour and make new ones. Put any cake bonbons that are ready back in the fridge to chill.

Melt the candy melts. Coat the cake bonbons by placing them in the candy melts, covering them with some more candy melts and then lifting them out with a fork. Tap the fork handle against the edge of the bowl to remove excess candy melts. Allow the bonbons to set on a sheet of greaseproof paper.

Add a thin layer of candy melts, using a cocktail stick, where you want to sprinkle some sugar, and sprinkle this on immediately. Attach the edible pearl on top of the bonbon with a small drop of candy melts.

WEDDING CAKE BONBON

INGREDIENTS

for 55 cake bonbons

*crumbled cake, mixed with
    frosting or butter cream (without
    rolling the cake into balls)*
1.2kg (3lb) violet candy melts
55 edible pink pearls

Also needed:
*bonbon mould, preferably a
    silicone mould*
greaseproof paper

Fill each hollow of the bonbon moulds with 20g (⅔oz) of cake mixture and repeat until you have used up all the cake. Chill the bonbons in the fridge for an hour. If you cannot use all the cake mixture in one go (if, for example, you only have one mould), then remove the cake bonbons from the mould after one hour and make new ones. Put any cake bonbons that are ready back in the fridge to chill.

Melt the candy melts. Coat the cake bonbons by placing them in the candy melts, covering them with some more candy melts and then lifting them out with a fork. Tap the fork handle against the edge of the bowl to remove excess candy melts. Allow the bonbons to set on a sheet of greaseproof paper and quickly but carefully attach the pink pearls, before the candy melts have set.

HEART CAKE BONBON

INGREDIENTS

for 55 cake bonbons

*crumbled cake, mixed with
    frosting or butter cream (without
    rolling the cake into balls)*
*300g (10½oz) red fondant or
    marzipan*
edible glue
edible red sugar
1.2kg (3lb) white candy melts

Also needed:
*bonbon mould, preferably a
    silicone mould*
heart mould
greaseproof paper

Fill each hollow of the bonbon moulds with 20g (⅔oz) of cake mixture and repeat until you have used up all the cake. Chill the bonbons in the fridge for an hour. If you cannot use all the cake mixture in one go (if, for example, you only have one mould), then remove the cake bonbons from the mould after one hour and make new ones. Put any cake bonbons that are ready back in the fridge to chill.

Fill the heart shape with red fondant or marzipan and push it out again. Make 55 hearts. Brush them with edible glue or a thin layer of candy melts and sprinkle on the red sugar.

Melt the candy melts. Coat the cake bonbons by placing them in the candy melts, covering them with some more candy melts and then lifting them out with a fork. Tap the fork handle against the edge of the bowl to remove excess candy melts. Allow the bonbons to set on a sheet of greaseproof paper and attach the heart. Make sure you do this before the coating has set.

MARITIME CUPCAKE POP

INGREDIENTS

for 55 cupcake pops

600g (21oz) blue candy melts
55 cake balls
600g (21oz) white candy melts
100g (3½oz) edible maritime
  sprinkles (fish, shells etc.)

Also needed:
peanut butter cup mould or a
  small cupcake bonbon mould
cocktail stick
55 lollipop sticks

Melt the blue candy melts. Fill the moulds halfway with coating, and place the cake ball on top. Carefully press the ball into the mould to coat it with the candy melts and give it a nice ridge. Make sure the coating doesn't spill over the edge, so stop as soon as this starts to happen. You will have to try out how much coating you need to spoon into the mould for the best results. Allow the cakes to set in the mould and then take them out.

Melt the white candy melts. Make a hole in the bottom of the blue part of each cupcake pop with a cocktail stick. Dip 2cm (¾in) of the lollipop sticks into the candy melts and push them halfway into the bottom of the cupcake pop (the blue part). Hold the cupcake pops by the lollipop stick and dip the top into the white coating, up to the blue edge.

Keep turning the cupcake while letting the excess coating drip off. Put the cupcake bonbon right side up and immediately sprinkle over the maritime sprinkles, before the candy melts have set.

INGREDIENTS

for 55 cupcake pops

600g (21oz) red candy melts
55 cake balls
600g (21oz) white candy melts
150g (5oz) fondant or marzipan
  (total weight), in the colours
  of your choice (at least 3)
tylose (gum or modelling paste)
  (optional)
55 edible pink pearls

Also needed:
peanut butter cup mould or
  small cupcake bonbon mould
cocktail stick
55 lollipop sticks
cutters (flower shapes)

FLOWER WITH BUTTERFLY CUPCAKE POP

Smelt the red candy melts. Fill the moulds halfway with coating and place the cake ball on top. Carefully press the ball into the mould, to coat it with the candy melts and give it a nice ridge. Make sure the coating doesn't spill over the edge, so stop as soon as this starts to happen. You will have to try out how much coating you need to spoon into the mould for the best results.

Allow the cakes to set in the mould and then take them out.

Melt the white candy melts. Make a hole in the bottom of the red part of each cupcake pop with a cocktail stick. Dip 2cm (¾in) of the lollipop sticks into the candy melts and push them halfway into the bottom of the cupcake pop (the red part). Dip the top of the cupcake pop into the white coating, up to the red edge. Keep turning the cupcake while letting the excess coating drip off.

Put the cupcake bonbon right side up and leave it to set. In the meantime, roll out the fondant or marzipan in the colours of your choice and cut out 3 sizes of flowers in various colours for each cupcake pop.

Place them on top of the cupcake and attach them with some candy melts (biggest at the bottom, smallest on top). Cut out 55 butterflies. If you want the wings to point up, mix in some tylose (gum or modelling paste) with the fondant or marzipan, put the butterflies in between two bits of folded paper and leave them to dry for at least 2 hours. Fold a thick sheet of paper lengthwise to make a W; you can place the butterflies in the folds, with the wings pointing up. When dry, attach the butterflies next to the flowers.

Stick an edible pearl on top of the flower for the flower heart.

ROSE CUPCAKE POP

Shape the cake balls into cupcakes by pushing them into a cupcake mould. I used a silicone mould for mini cupcakes. Chill the cakes in the fridge for an hour. If you cannot use all the cake mixture in one go (if, for example, you only have one mould), then remove the cupcakes from the mould after one hour and make new ones. Put any cupcakes that are ready back in the fridge to chill.

Melt the candy melts. Dip 2cm (¾in) of the lollipop sticks into the candy melts and push them halfway into the cupcakes. Dip the cake pops into the candy melts and allow them to set.

In the meantime, use the rose mould to make little red roses from the fondant or marzipan. (If you don't have a flower mould, you can use ready-made sugarpaste roses.)

Stick the roses on top of the cupcakes using some candy melts. Use a brush to cover the pops and roses with pink glitter dust.

INGREDIENTS

for 55 cake pops

55 cake balls
1.2kg (3lb) pink candy melts
250g (9oz) red fondant or marzipan
edible pink glitter dust

Also needed:
cupcake mould
rose mould
55 lollipop sticks
brush

EASTER BUNNY CAKE POP

Melt the pink and white candy melts (separately). Dip 2cm (¾in) of the lollipop sticks into the candy melts and push them halfway into the cake balls. Dip half of the cake pops into the pink candy melts and the other half in the white candy melts. Allow them to set.

Roll out the fondant or marzipan (keep it quite thick) and cut out 2 large ears per cake pop, and two smaller ears per cake pop from the other colour. Stick the smaller ears onto the larger ears. Dip the bottom of the ears into the candy melts and attach them to the bunny heads. Hold on to the ears until the melts have set and the ears are attached.

Attach a small white or pink hart as a nose. Dip a cocktail stick into the white candy melts to make eyes and mouths on the pink bunnies, doing the same with pink candy melts on the white bunnies.

INGREDIENTS

for 55 cake pops

600g (21oz) pink candy melts
600g (21oz) white candy melts
55 cake balls
100g (3½oz) pink fondant or marzipan
100g (3½oz) white fondant or marzipan
55 small white and/or pink hearts

Also needed:
55 lollipop sticks
rose mould
cocktail stick

EASTER CHICK CAKE POP

Melt the candy melts. Dip 2cm (¾in) of the lollipop sticks into the candy melts and push them halfway into the cake balls. Dip half of the cake pops into the candy melts and allow them to set.

Roll out the fondant or marzipan (keep it quite thick) and cut out 4 small hearts per cake pop. Attach 2 yellow hearts, overlapping to form a wing, and stick these on the sides of the chicken. Insert a red heart into the candy melts for the beak and attach 2 red hearts to the bottom for the legs. Make 2 small black balls per cake pop for the eyes and use some candy melts to attach them. Dip the small white hearts in the candy melts and stick 3 of these hearts on top of each cake pop.

INGREDIENTS

for 55 cake pops

1.2kg (3lb) yellow candy melts
55 cake balls
50g (1¾oz) yellow fondant
  or marzipan
165 small, edible red hearts
10 g black fondant or marzipan
165 small, edible white hearts

Also needed:
55 lollipop sticks
small heart cutter

SNOWMAN CAKE POP

Melt the candy melts. Dip 2cm (¾in) of the lollipop sticks into the candy melts. Push 1 cakeball all the way over the stick and then push the stick halfway into a second cake ball. Dip the cake pops into the candy melts and allow them to set.

Roll out the fondant or marzipan in the colour(s) of your choice thinly and cut out 25 wide strips for the scarf.

Score the ends, to make fringes. Wrap the scarf around the snowman's neck and attach it with some candy melts.

Roll carrot noses from the orange fondant or marzipan and score them a bit to make grooves. Dip the fat end of each carrot into the candy melts and attach to the face.

From the black fondant or marzipan, roll 4 small balls for each snowman and attach 2 as eyes and 2 as buttons. Make a larger ball from the black fondant or marzipan, shape this into a hat and attach it on top of the head. You can use edible ink to draw on a mouth.

INGREDIENTS

for 25 cake pops

1.2kg (3lb) white candy melts
50 cake balls
50g (1¾oz) fondant or marzipan,
  in the colours of your choice
25g ¾oz) orange fondant or marzipan
100g (3½oz) black fondant or
  marzipan with tylose (gum
  or modelling paste)

edible ink (optional)

Also needed:
25 lollipop sticks

CAKE POP BY CANDLELIGHT

Take around 20g (⅔oz) of cake mixture and make a candle shape. Repeat until you have used up all the cake. Chill the candles in the fridge for an hour. Melt the candy melts. Dip 2cm (¾in) of the lollipop sticks into the candy melts and push them halfway into the cake pops. Dip the cake pops into the candy melts and allow them to set.

Spoon some candy melts over the candle and pull it down in places, to make it look like melting candle wax. Put a drop-shaped candy on top for the flame.

INGREDIENTS

for 55 cake pops

crumbled cake, mixed with
  frosting or butter cream
  without rolling the cake into balls)
1.2kg (3lb) white candy melts
55 edible drop-shaped candies for
the flames

Also needed:
55 lollipop sticks

SANTA HAT CAKE POP

Take 20g (⅔oz) of cake mixture and push this into the hollows of a cone mould. Repeat until you have used up all the cake. Chill the cones in the fridge for an hour. Remove the cones from the mould. If you cannot use all the cake mixture in one go (if, for example, you only have one mould), then remove the cones from the mould after one hour and make new ones. Put any cones that are ready back in the fridge to chill.

Melt the candy melts. Dip 2cm (¾in) of the lollipop sticks into the candy melts and push them halfway into the cake pops. Dip the cake pops into the candy melts (see Coating the cakeballs). Press a white rice candy on top immediately.

Use a cocktail stick to brush on some candy melts to the bottom edge of the cone and sprinkle on some sugar glitter.

Allow the hats to set.

INGREDIENTS

for 55 cake pops

crumbled cake, mixed with
    frosting or butter cream (without
    rolling the cake into balls)
1.2kg (3lb) red candy melts
55 small white rice candy
50g (1¾oz) edible white
    sugar glitter

Also needed:
cone mould
55 lollipop sticks
cocktail stick

CHRISTMAS TREE CAKE POP

Take 20g (⅔oz) of cake mixture and push this into the hollows of a cone mould. Repeat until you have used up all the cake. Chill the cones in the fridge for an hour. Remove the cones from the mould. If you cannot use all the cake mixture in one go (if, for example, you only have one mould), then remove the cones from the mould after one hour and make new ones. Put any cones that are ready back in the fridge to chill.

Melt the candy melts. Dip 2cm (¾in) of the lollipop sticks into the candy melts and push them halfway into the cake pops. Dip the cake pops into the candy melts and decorate them with the green sugar glitter immediately. Use a cocktail stick to put some candy melts on the tip of the Christmas tree and attach a star.

INGREDIENTS

for 55 cake pops

crumbled cake, mixed with
   frosting or butter cream (without
   rolling the cake into balls)
1.2kg (3lb) green candy melts
150g (5oz) green sugar glitters
55 edible star candies

Also needed:
cone mould
55 lollipop sticks
cocktail stick

Published in 2012 by New Holland Publishers
London • Sydney • Auckland • Cape Town
www.newholland.com.au
www.newhollandpublishers.com

1/66 Gibbes Street Chatswood NSW 2067 Australia
218 Lake Road Northcote Auckland New Zealand
86 Edgware Road London W2 2EA United Kingdom
Wembly Square First Floor Solan Road Gardens Cape Town 8001

First published in 2011 by Veltman Uitgevers
Copyright © 2012 New Holland Publishers

Text, recipes and food styling: Francis van Arkel, NutriVisie
Styling: Lize Boer (www.lize-b.nl)
Photography: Remco Lassche (Bart Nijs Fotografie)
Translation: Ammerins Moss-de Boer, Leeuwarden, Ammerins Moss/Vitataal
Design and cover: Studio Buskruit, Den Ham
Production Director: Olga Dementiev
Printed by Toppan Leefung (China) Ltd
www.veltman-uitgevers.nl

A word of thanks to:
Intratuin (www.intratuin.nl)
And a special thank-you to my mom, Toos Kuipers, for the many inspirational and fun hours we've spent
together, thinking up and making the Cake Pops in this book!

10 9 8 7 6 5 4 3
Follow New Holland Publishers on Facebook: www.facebook.com/NewHollandPublishers